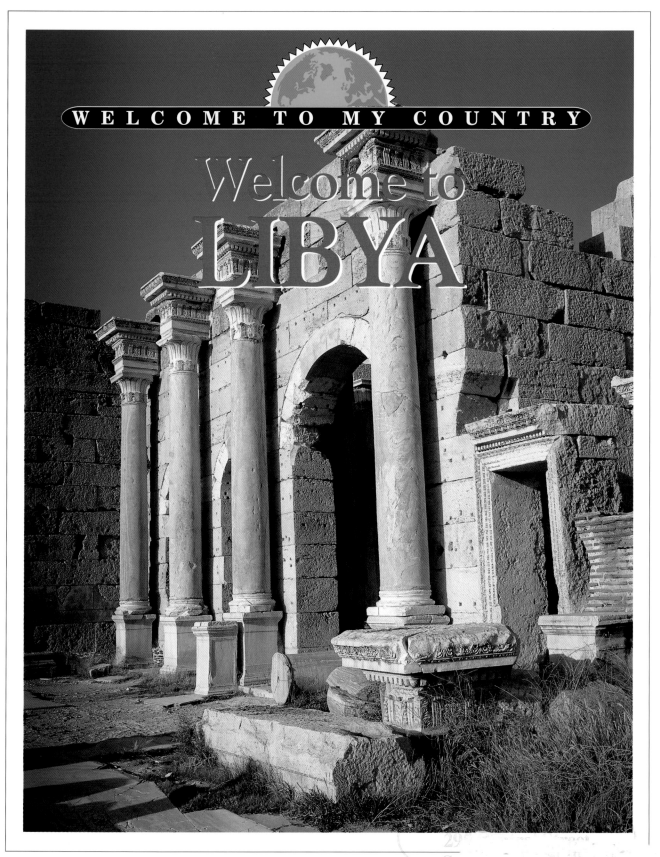

WELCOME TO MY COUNTRY

Welcome to LIBYA

Gareth Stevens Publishing
A WORLD ALMANAC EDUCATION GROUP COMPANY

Written by
RONALD TAN

Edited by
MELVIN NEO

Edited in USA by
JENETTE DONOVAN GUNTLY

Designed by
GEOSLYN LIM

Picture research by
SUSAN JANE MANUEL
THOMAS KHOO

First published in North America in 2005 by
Gareth Stevens Publishing
A World Almanac Education Group Company
330 West Olive Street, Suite 100
Milwaukee, Wisconsin 53212 USA

Please visit our web site at
www.garethstevens.com
For a free color catalog describing
Gareth Stevens Publishing's list of high-quality
books and multimedia programs,
call 1-800-542-2595 (USA) or
1-800-387-3178 (Canada).
Gareth Stevens Publishing's fax: (414) 332-3567.

© **MARSHALL CAVENDISH INTERNATIONAL (ASIA)**
PRIVATE LIMITED 2005
Originated and designed by
Times Editions Marshall Cavendish
An imprint of Marshall Cavendish International (Asia) Pte Ltd
A member of Times Publishing Limited
Times Centre, 1 New Industrial Road
Singapore 536196
http://www.marshallcavendish.com/genref

Library of Congress Cataloging-in-Publication Data
Tan, Ronald.
Welcome to Libya / Ronald Tan.
p. cm. — (Welcome to my country)
Includes bibliographical references and index.
ISBN 0-8368-3129-2 (lib. bdg.)
1. Libya—Juvenile literature. I. Title. II. Series.
DT215.T36   2005
961.2—dc22   2004052496

Printed in Singapore

1 2 3 4 5 6 7 8 9 09 08 07 06 05

PICTURE CREDITS
Agence French Presse: 19, 36 (both),
    37 (both)
ANA Press Agency: 3 (center), 8, 27,
    30 (bottom), 43, 45
Art Directors & TRIP Photo Library: cover,
    5, 9 (top), 20, 21, 23, 24, 25, 32, 39
Focus Team Italy: 2, 3 (top & bottom), 26,
    28, 31, 33, 40, 41
Getty Images/Hulton Archive: 13 (bottom),
    17, 18
The Hutchison Picture Library: 6, 7,
    9 (bottom), 22, 38
John R. Jones: 1, 4, 10, 11, 13 (top),
    14, 29 (top)
Lonely Planet Images: 16, 29 (bottom),
    30 (top), 34
Audrius Tomonis—www.banknotes.com:
    44 (both)
Topham Picturepoint: 12, 15 (both), 35

Digital Scanning by Superskill Graphics Pte Ltd

Contents

Words that appear in the glossary are printed in **boldface** type the first time they occur in the text.

Welcome to Libya!

Libya is an **ancient** land located on the coast of North Africa. The country's art, architecture, and religion have been influenced by many of the land's past rulers, including the Greeks, Romans, and Ottomans. Let's visit Libya and learn about its long, rich history and its interesting people!

Opposite: The town of Ghadames, in the northwest of Libya, is very old. In desert areas, many people paint walls white. The white walls help keep buildings cool.

Below: Libyans like to spend time with their families and friends. They often visit at tea shops.

The Flag of Libya

Since Libya became **independent** in 1951, the country has had three flags. The current flag of Libya was adopted in 1977. It is solid green. The color green is a symbol of loyalty to the Islamic religion.

The Land

Libya has a land area of 679,362 square miles (1,759,540 square kilometers). To the north of Libya is the Mediterranean Sea. To the east, south, and west of the country are the nations of Egypt, Sudan, Chad, Niger, Algeria, and Tunisia. The country's highest point is a peak in the Tibesti Mountains called Bikku Bitti. It is 7,438 feet (2,267 meters) high.

Below: A few parts of Libya have rocky outcroppings or **plateaus,** but most of the country is made up of flat or rolling deserts.

Libya's Regions

The land in Libya is divided into three regions. Tripolitania is the northwestern region. Most of the land is covered in **terraces** and plains. Jabal Nafusah, a high plateau, is also in this area. The region has many **oases**, which make it Libya's best farmland. Cyrenaica is the eastern region. The southern part of this region is covered by the Sahara Plateau, which is a desert area with some oases. Fezzan is in the southwest. Long, high sand dunes cover most of this region.

Above: Oases are a welcome sight for travelers in Libya. They may offer the only clean drinking water in the long stretches of the country's deserts.

7

Climate

In the north, along Libya's coast, the summers are warm and the winters are cool. In Tripolitania, temperatures in the summertime can climb as high as 115° Fahrenheit (46° Celsius). Winter temperatures average 52° F (11° C). Summer temperatures in the southern regions average 100° F (38° C). Winter temperatures average 63° F (17° C). Libya gets very little rain, especially in the southern regions. Some desert areas get no rainfall.

Above: Plants grow up to the walls of the ancient city of Sabratha in the Tripolitania region. The climate along the coast is milder than in other areas of Libya, making it possible for some plants to survive.

Plants and Animals

Much of Libya is hot and dry, so few plants can grow. Some plants, such as henna plants, pistachio trees, and date palms, grow near oases. Grassy plains called steppes used to stretch across the northern regions. Most of these steppes are now used for farmland.

Above: A few hardy plants are able to survive in the harsh climate of Libya's desert regions.

Many kinds of animals live in Libya, including foxes, gazelles, guinea pigs, leopards, and wildcats. Some birds also live in Libya, including vultures, eagles, and prairie hens. The country has many insects, including swarms of locusts and butterflies. Libyans often raise animals such as camels, goats, cows, and sheep.

Left: Reptiles, such as lizards (*left*), are a common sight in the deserts of Libya. Chameleons and poisonous snakes also live in Libya's desert regions.

History

In what is now Libya, scientists have found **settlements** that date back to between 8000 and 6000 B.C. During that time, **savannas** covered the land in the south. When the land turned into deserts, the groups living there moved toward the coast or to desert oases. The Berbers, who were from Asia, moved to the region between 2700 and 2200 B.C. In about 600 B.C., the Phoenicians came across the sea to settle in the northwest. During that century, the Greeks began to arrive. They settled in the northeast.

Left: This ancient theater was built in Sabratha. The city was one of three settlements created by the Phoenicians. They also founded Lepcis, which is now called Leptis Magna, and Oea, which is now the city of Tripoli.

Left: Many ancient settlements, such as Yafran in the Tripolitania region, were built on high ground. Being on top of a hill helped the town's citizens spot invaders as they approached.

The Romans and the Arabs

By 96 B.C., the Romans had taken over the northwest of the country from the Phoenicians. They also took control of the northeast from the Greeks. The Romans brought the Christian religion to North Africa. Groups of Arabs from Saudi Arabia **invaded** the land in the seventh century A.D. They brought the religion of Islam with them. More Arab groups arrived in the eleventh century. Islamic **dynasties** ruled the region from the ninth to the sixteenth centuries.

The Ottoman Turks

In 1551, present-day Libya was taken over by the Ottomans, who were from Turkey. They chose an official called a *bey* (BAY) from a local tribe. The bey governed the region and collected taxes for the Ottomans. In 1711, the region's bey, Ahmad Qaramanli, took control from the Ottomans. His family ruled the area until 1835. Then the Ottomans took back the land. An Islamic group called the Sanusiyah formed in 1837. They fought against the Ottomans.

Left: This picture shows two Tuareg people meeting in the deserts of what is now Libya. The Tuareg are believed to be **descendants** of the Berbers who settled in the area of southwest Libya.

The Italians and Independence

In 1911, during World War I, Italy took over many Ottoman lands, including present-day Libya. The Sanusiyah and other groups fought the Italians. In response, the Italians put entire tribes in prison camps. They also took farmland and gave it to Italians. After World War II, the region was taken away from the Italians. Libya became independent on December 24, 1951. King Idris I of the Sanusiyah ruled the land. He was taken out of power on September 1, 1969, and Libya was declared a **republic**.

Above: The Tobruk Commonwealth War Cemetery is located in the northeast of Libya, near Egypt. During World War II, several important battles were fought in the region.

Libya and Colonel al-Qadhafi

In 1969, Colonel Mu'ammar al-Qadhafi led the fight to take King Idris I out of power. He then became Libya's leader. Over several decades, countries around the world accused al-Qadhafi and his government of supporting **terrorists**. In 1992 and 1993, the **United Nations (UN)** put **sanctions** on Libya because the country refused to hand over two Libyan men. The men were accused of blowing up an airplane over Lockerbie, Scotland. In 1999, Libya gave up the men. In 2003, the sanctions were lifted.

Left: Posters of Colonel al-Qadhafi hang all over Libya. Since he became leader in 1969, al-Qadhafi has tried to make Libya more powerful. Libya took over a part of Chad for a time and has tried to gain power in other countries in North Africa as well.

Septimius Severus (A.D. 145–211)

Septimius Severus was born in what is now Libya. In A.D. 193, he became a Roman emperor. During his rule, he improved ports and constructed many buildings. Some of the **ruins** of these buildings can still be seen in Libya.

Septimius Severus

Omar al-Mukhtar (1862–1931)

Omar al-Mukhtar led the Sanusiyah. He believed that it was every Libyan's duty to fight against foreign control of the country. He was able to gather many tribes to fight the Italians. In 1931, the Italians captured and later killed him.

Mu'ammar al-Qadhafi (1942–)

Mu'ammar al-Qadhafi was born to desert **nomads**. In 1963, he graduated from the University of Libya. He later joined the military. Al-Qadhafi took over the country in 1969. Although he has no official title, today he rules as chief of state and head of the military.

Mu'ammar al-Qadhafi

Government and the Economy

Libya was renamed the Great Socialist People's Libyan Arab Jamahiriya in 1977. At that time, the General People's Congress (GPC) was formed to run the government and make laws. The GPC is headed by the General Secretariat and the General People's Committee. The official head of the Libyan government is the secretary of the General People's Committee. Mu'ammar al-Qadhafi still unofficially runs the country, however.

Left: The Central Bank of Libya is located in Tripoli, which is Libya's capital city.

Left: Even though Colonel al-Qadhafi (*right*) does not hold an official position, he is still Libya's chief of state. In that role, he meets with leaders from other African nations. In 1972, he attended a meeting along with Algeria's president, Houari Boumediene (*left*), and Egypt's president, Anwar Sadat (*center*).

Local Government

Libya has twenty-five *baladiyat* (bah-lah-DEE-yaht), or government regions. In these regions, each town, city, and village has a Basic People's Congress. The congresses are groups that run local government with the help of officials.

The Legal System

Libya's legal system is based mainly on the laws of the Islamic religion. The laws are called *shari'ah* (sha-REE-yah). The Supreme Court is Libya's highest court. It deals with **appeals** and cases about Libya's laws and **constitution**.

The Economy

Libya's economy depends mostly on oil, which was found in the country in 1959. In 2003, the country produced more than one million barrels of oil a day. Oil has made Libya one of the richest nations in Africa. Libya earns a lot of money from producing oil and from selling oil to foreign countries. Since the United Nations lifted its sanctions in 2003, Libya is expected to sell even more oil to other nations.

Left: In the late 1950s, the Esso Standard Company began working in Libya. It was one of the first foreign oil companies to come to the country. Now, most oil companies in Libya are run by the government.

Farming and Other Industries

Before oil was found in Libya, most people worked in farming. Today, few Libyans work as farmers. The country must **import** most of its food. A few crops are still grown, including wheat, olives, vegetables, peanuts, and dates.

Other industries include mining and manufacturing. Libya's mining industry mainly focuses on mining oil. Minerals such as sulphur, gypsum, potash, and salt are also mined. Besides **refining** oil, some manufacturers in Libya make cloth, cement, or food products.

People and Lifestyle

Most Libyan people have Arab-Berber **ancestors**. Smaller groups of Libyans have ancestors from Greece, Pakistan, Malta, Italy, Egypt, Turkey, India, or Tunisia. A small number of people in Libya are Africans who have come to the country to work. Libya has one of Africa's fastest growing populations. Because it has grown so fast, many Libyans are under fourteen years old. Most Libyans are under age sixty-four.

Left: Most Libyans live in city areas. Many of them live in the capital city of Tripoli. Many Libyans also live in Benghazi, which is the country's second-largest city.

Families

In Libya, it is very important to most people to know which clan, or tribe, they belong to. Some of the clans were started hundreds of years ago. A *sheikh* (SHAKE) leads each clan. Within the clan are separate family groups called *bayt* (BAIT). The bayt includes great-grandparents, grandparents, parents, children, aunts, uncles, and cousins. In the countryside, the bayt usually live in one house or in a group of houses. In the city, the bayt may live in the same apartment building or neighborhood.

Traditional Lifestyles

Most Libyans live in cities and have modern lifestyles. Some small groups in the countryside, including the Berbers, Bedouin, and Tuareg, have **traditional** lifestyles. The Berbers speak their own language and Arabic. They still follow Berber laws and practices. The Bedouin are desert nomads who move from oasis to oasis with their camels and goats. In Tuareg tribes, women hold a high place. They own all of the tents and animals.

Below: Although some Tuareg people still live in Libya's deserts, many of them have moved to towns and villages.

Left: In the past, most Libyan women were expected to stay home and care for their families. Today, women are encouraged to hold jobs outside of their homes. Women are also able to serve in Libya's army.

Women in Libya

In Libya, women have always been an important part of society. In the past, women's roles were mainly to marry, raise children, and care for the home. In 1969, Libyan women were given full rights, including the right to vote. The government encouraged women to get an education. Day care centers were opened and women were given money to return to work after having children. Today, because of these changes, many Libyan women are professionals.

Education

In elementary school, Libyan children must study math, the Arabic language, science, the arts, and the Qur'an, which is the holy book of the Islamic religion. After three years of elementary school, boys may attend a school to study the Qur'an. During the six years the boys attend the program, they talk about and memorize the Qur'an and other Islamic texts. They also receive an education in regular school subjects.

Below:
In Libya, children begin elementary school at age six. They attend school for nine years. Some children also attend preschool at age four or five.

Left: Schoolgirls walk through the streets of Sabha in western Libya. After they finish elementary school, many students choose to attend secondary school, although they are not required to.

Secondary Schools and Universities

After elementary school, students may attend secondary school, which lasts up to four years. During secondary school, all students receive military training.

After secondary school, students may attend a university. Study programs last from three to six years. The University of Libya was founded in Benghazi in 1955. It was Libya's first university. In 1972, the university was split into Al-Fatah University in Tripoli and the University of Garyounis in Benghazi.

Religion

Islam is Libya's official religion. The followers of Islam are called Muslims. Almost all Libyans are Muslims. The rest of the people are mostly Christians.

Islam was founded by Muhammad, who was a **prophet**. Muslims believe Allah, or God, spoke the holy Qur'an directly to Muhammad. Islam has two main groups, the Sunni and the Shiite. Most Libyans are Sunni Muslims.

Below: Libya has many mosques, which are Islamic houses of worship. Friday is the main prayer day for all Muslims. On Friday, most Muslim men and women go to pray in mosques. They must pray in separate parts of the building.

Left: These men are reading the Qur'an, the holy book of the Islamic religion. It is written in classical Arabic. The Qur'an has not changed since it was written down for the first time during the seventh century.

Islam in Daily Life

Islam influences the daily life of most Libyans because the country's laws are based on the laws of the Qur'an. Also, Muslims are expected to live by the Five Pillars of Islam, a set of religious rules. The first rule is to recite, "There is no God but Allah, and Muhammad is His messenger." The other pillars are to pray five times a day, to donate money to the poor, not to eat during daylight hours in the holy month of Ramadan, and to make at least one **pilgrimage** to the holy city of Mecca in Saudi Arabia.

Language

Arabic is Libya's official language. It is used in the government and in business. Arabic is also used in schools. Libyans who live in cities may speak Italian or English. Often, in large cities, English is taught at schools. Other languages in the nation include Tamazight, which is spoken by the Berbers and the Tuareg.

In Libya, newspapers are printed in the Arabic language. Some newspapers also have English-language editions.

Below:
Signs in Libya are often printed in both Arabic and English. Arabic writing is made up of many loops and swirls.

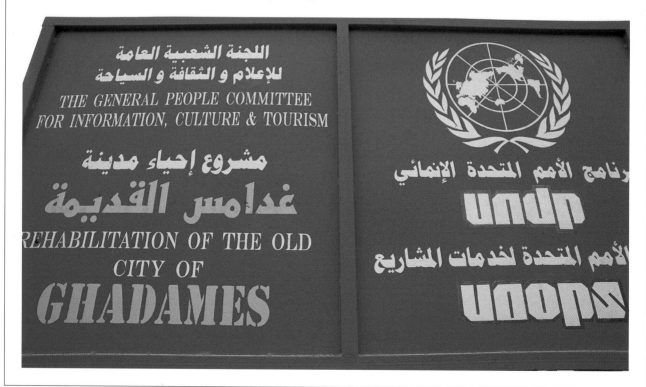

اللجنة الشعبية العامة
للإعلام و الثقافة و السياحة

THE GENERAL PEOPLE COMMITTEE
FOR INFORMATION, CULTURE & TOURISM

مشروع إحياء مدينة
غدامس القديمة

REHABILITATION OF THE OLD
CITY OF
GHADAMES

رنامج الأمم المتحدة الإنمائي

undp

الأمم المتحدة لخدمات المشاريع

unops

Left: A young girl practices writing simple words in the Arabic language. Children in Libya learn how to read and write Arabic in elementary school.

Literature

Bedouin poetry is a popular form of literature in Libya. Many of the poems have been written down only in the last one hundred years. Before that, poems were spoken out loud and passed from person to person. Most Bedouin poetry is sung. People clap and play drums to keep the rhythm. One famous Bedouin poet in Libya is Sheikh Rajib Buhwaish al-Manfi. He wrote about cruelty in an Italian prison camp.

Below: In the 1970s, Colonel al-Qadhafi wrote *The Green Book*. It talks about his ideas for how the government of Libya should work.

Arts

Architecture

Libya has many styles of architecture that show the country's long history. The ruins of ancient Roman towns still stand in Tripolitania, including Leptis Magna and Sabratha. In Cyrenaica, Roman and Greek ruins can be found. Libya also has many beautiful Islamic mosques. They usually have tall towers called minarets and large prayer halls.

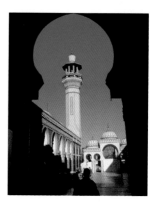

Above: Many of Libya's mosques are decorated with ceramic tiles and beautiful stone and wood carvings.

Left:
The ancient Roman city of Leptis Magna was built more than two thousand years ago. The Romans built temples, baths, theaters, and other buildings. Many of the ruins of these buildings still exist.

Berber Architecture

Berber architecture is well known in Libya. The *qasr* (KAH-ser), or castle, is the main type of Berber building. The castles were built in the Jabal Nafusah area in the 1100s. The Berbers used the qasr as protection against their enemies. The buildings were also used as storage spaces for food, including olive oil and grain. Today, near Jadu, some Berbers live underground. Their homes have courtyards and rooms carved from rock.

Above: Many Libyan homes are built with central courtyards. The courtyards let in lots of fresh air and sunlight. Some wealthy Libyans have fountains built in their courtyards.

Music and Dance

Music and dance are a part of many events in Libya. At weddings, Libyans often perform *malouf* (muh-LOOF), in which groups of people sing religious and love poems. At New Year festivals, many Tuareg women play drums and sing songs about Tuareg heroes. While they sing, men ride camels around the women in a circle. Traditional Libyan instruments include the *nay* (NAH-ee), a kind of flute, and the *gheeta* (HEE-tah), which is similar to a clarinet.

Left:
These singers are wearing traditional Libyan costumes. While they sing, they play drums to keep the rhythm.

Libyan Crafts

People from all over Libya make crafts. Crafts made in cities include wooden marriage chests, leather crafts, copper pots, and pottery. Jewelers in cities are known for fancy gold jewelry, which women often wear at weddings. The Tuareg and the Berbers are known for silver jewelry. The Berbers also make colorful cloth, which they often use to create traditional clothing and veils.

Leisure

Most Libyans like to spend leisure time with family and friends. Many Libyans watch television. Many of them like to listen to the radio, too. Attending soccer games and going to festivals and to the theater are also popular.

In Libya, board and card games are very popular. One favorite card game is *romeeno* (roh-MEEN-oh). It is a kind of gin rummy. *Kharbga* (KARB-gah) is a traditional board game in which the two players try to win the most game pieces.

Left: During the day, if they have any free time, Libyan men often visit with male friends and family members. In the evenings and on weekends, Libyan men often listen to the radio or watch television at home with their families.

Vacations

Many Libyans like to go on vacation, especially on weekends and during the summer. Because the government has placed limits on traveling outside of the country, most Libyans take vacations inside Libya. They often visit one of the tourist villages built by the government. The tourist villages usually have hotels, restaurants, activity centers, and game rooms. Many of the villages were built along the beautiful and famous beaches that line Libya's coast. Some villages were also built in the countryside.

Soccer

Soccer is Libya's most popular sport. Many Libyans enjoy playing soccer or watching soccer matches. The country has many local soccer teams. Three well-known teams include Al-Madina, Al-Ahly, and Al-Ittihad. Well-known players include Tariq al-Taib and Jihad al-Muntasser. The country's national team plays against teams from African nations and countries around the world.

Above left: During the first Arab Clubs' Competition, which was held in Saudi Arabia in 2003, Adel Shatawi (*right*) and Nadr Karah (*left*), of Libya, tried to keep the ball from Saudi Arabia's Hamza Idris (*center*).

Above right: In another soccer game, Aravi Bin Yousek (*right*) of Libya fights for control of the ball from Hamdi al-Marzouk of Tunisia.

Other Sports

In Tripoli and Benghazi, Libyans play basketball, handball, and volleyball at large sports centers. The country has many sports societies, including the Libyan National Olympic Committee, the Libyan Volleyball Federation, and the Libyan Tennis Federation. Women often play table tennis and volleyball.

In southern Libya and other areas of the countryside, camel and horse racing are popular. Some Bedouin tribes enjoy hunting with *salukis* (suh-LOO-kees), or fast, graceful desert greyhounds.

Above: In 2003, soccer star Saadi al-Qadhafi, who is Colonel al-Qadhafi's son, was given the chance to train with Perugia, an Italian soccer team. Today, a growing number of talented Libyan soccer players are joining teams in foreign countries.

Left: In 2003, the Libyan government hosted the Paris-Dakar Motor **Rally**. The international car race passed through the city of Ghadames in northwestern Libya.

Religious Festivals

Many of Libya's festivals are religious. During each day of Ramadan, which is the Islamic holy month, most Muslims do not eat or drink until sunset. *Id al Saghir* (EED ahl suh-GEER) celebrates the end of Ramadan. The festival lasts several days. Before the festival begins, people buy clothes and gifts for their friends and families. On the morning of Id al Saghir, families pray at mosques. Then they enjoy large meals with their family members and friends at home.

Left: These men and boys in Ghadames have gathered for prayers before they eat at sunset during Ramadan, which is Islam's holy month.

Left: During the festival of Eid al-Adha, many Libyans kill and roast a ram. They eat it during a traditional meal to honor this event.

Two months after Id al Saghir is *Eid al-Adha* (EED al-AD-ha). The festival honors Abraham, who was willing to obey Allah's orders to kill his own son. The Qur'an says Allah stopped him and told Abraham to kill a ram instead.

National Holidays

Libya has nonreligious holidays as well. The most important national holiday in Libya is Revolution Day, which falls on September 1. In Tripoli and Benghazi, Libyans celebrate the holiday with large rallies, military parades, and speeches by Colonel al-Qadhafi.

Food

Libyan food is a mix of Middle Eastern and Mediterranean cooking. In coastal cities, Italian cooking is very popular. Traditional Libyan cooking is common mostly in southern Libya.

Couscous (koos-koos) is a favorite dish made of boiled millet, wheat, or barley. It is served with potatoes and meats, such as chicken. *Bazin* (buh-ZEEN) is a flatbread made of barley.

Left:
Shurba (SHOOR-bah) is a traditional Libyan dish. It is a flavorful and spicy soup made of lamb, onions, tomatoes, lemon, pepper, oil, and cinnamon.

Bureek (BOO-reek) are tasty Libyan turnovers. They are filled with many kinds of stuffing, including meat, eggs, spinach, or potatoes. One popular dish is *tajeen* (tah-JEEN). It is made with lamb, tomatoes, and paprika, which is a spice. *Rishda* (REESH-dah) is also a favorite. It is made by mixing noodles with tomatoes, chickpeas, and onions.

Many Libyans enjoy *matruda* (mah-TROO-dah), a dessert of bread pieces and dates in milk, butter, and honey.

Above: Markets in Libya sell many kinds of fruits and vegetables, such as tomatoes, dates, and lentils.

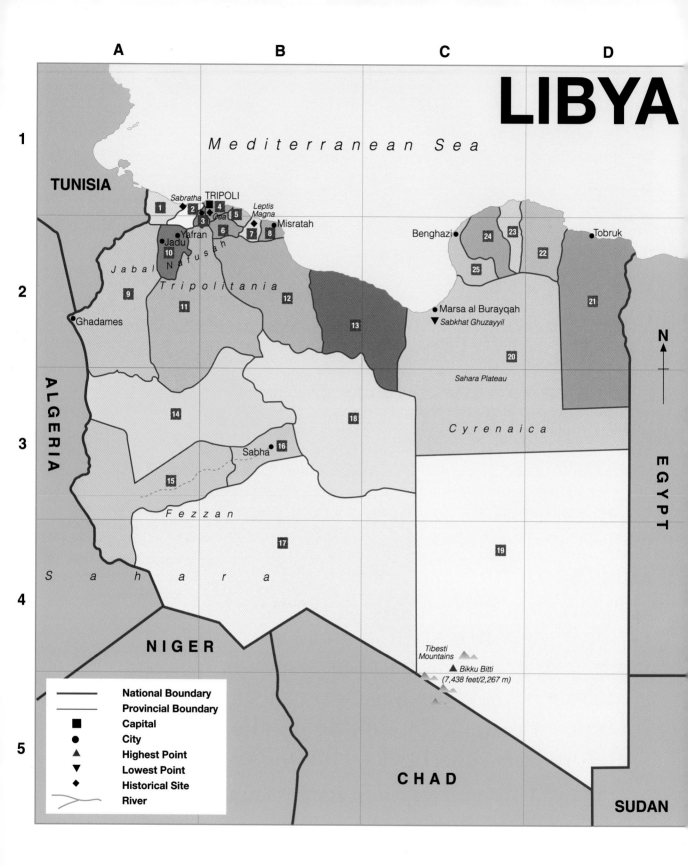

LIBYA

M e d i t e r r a n e a n   S e a

TUNISIA

Sabratha TRIPOLI

1

2 Cea 4 5 Leptis Magna

3 6 7 8 Misratah

Yafran

Jadu 10

J a b a l   N a f u s a h

9

11

Ghadames

T r i p o l i t a n i a

12

13

Benghazi 24 23

25 22 Tobruk

Marsa al Burayqah

Sabkhat Ghuzayyil

21

20

Sahara Plateau

C y r e n a i c a

14

18

Sabha 16

15

F e z z a n

19

17

S a h a r a

ALGERIA

EGYPT

N

N I G E R

Tibesti Mountains

▲ Bikku Bitti
(7,438 feet/2,267 m)

——	**National Boundary**
—	**Provincial Boundary**
■	**Capital**
●	**City**
▲	**Highest Point**
▼	**Lowest Point**
◆	**Historical Site**
～	**River**

C H A D

SUDAN

BALADIYAH

1. An Nuqat Al Khams
2. Az Zawiyah
3. Al 'Aziziyah
4. Tarabulus
5. Al Khums
6. Tarhunah
7. Zlitan
8. Misratah
9. Ghadames
10. Yafran
11. Gharyan
12. Sawfajun
13. Sirte
14. Ash Shati
15. Awbari
16. Sabha
17. Murzuq
18. Al Jufrah
19. Al Kufrah
20. Ajdabiya
21. Tobruk
22. Derna
23. Al Jabal Al Akhdar
24. Al Fatih
25. Benghazi

Above: Palm trees and plants crowd around the precious water of a desert oasis.

Algeria A2–A5

Benghazi C2
Bikku Bitti C4

Chad B4–D5
Cyrenaica C1–D3

Egypt D2–D4

Fezzan A3–B4

Ghadames A2

Jabal Nafusah
   A2–B2
Jadu A2

Leptis Magna B2

Marsa al
   Burayqah C2
Mediterranean Sea
   A1–D2

Misratah B2

Niger A4–B5

Oea B1

Sabha B3
Sabkhat
   Ghuzayyil C2
Sabratha A1
Sahara Desert
   A3–D5

Sahara Plateau C3
Sudan D5

Tibesti
   Mountains C4
Tobruk D2
Tripoli B1
Tripolitania A1–B2
Tunisia A1–A2

Yafran A2

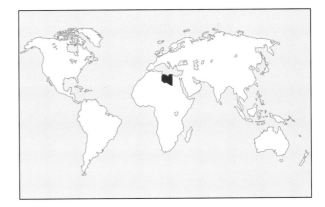

43

Quick Facts

Official Name	Great Socialist People's Libyan Arab Jamahiriya
Capital	Tripoli
Official Language	Arabic
Official Religion	Islam
Population	5,499,074 (July 2003 estimate)
Land Area	679,362 square miles (1,759,540 sq km)
Highest Point	Bikku Bitti 7,438 feet (2,267 m)
Lowest Point	Sabkhat Ghuzayyil 154 feet (47 m) below sea level
Coastline	1,110 miles (1,785 km)
Major Cities	Tripoli, Benghazi, Misratah, Sabha
Major Holidays	Declaration of the People's Authority Day (March 2), Evacuation Day (March 28, June 11, October 7), Revolution Day (September 1), Day of Mourning (October 26)
Famous Leaders	Septimius Severus (A.D. 145–211), Ahmad Qaramanli (c. 1711–1845), Omar al-Mukhtar (1862–1931), Mu'ammar al-Qadhafi (1942–)
Currency	Libyan Dinar (LYD 1.34 = U.S. $1 as of July 2004)

Opposite: The ancient and beautiful ruins of Leptis Magna are famous around the world.

Glossary

alliances: formal agreements to work together for a specific reason.

ancestors: family members from the past, farther back than grandparents.

ancient: relating to being very old.

appeals: the bringing of legal cases to a higher court to be heard over again.

constitution: written rules for a nation.

descendants: people born in a recent generation to one group or family.

dynasties: series of rulers from one family who rule over a long period.

import (verb): to buy and ship goods into a country from other countries.

independent: relating to being free from control by others.

invaded: entered a region by force to take land or valuable objects.

nomads: people who move from place to place and who often live in tents.

oases: areas in desert regions where there is water and plants can grow.

pilgrimage: a journey made to a holy place as an act of religious devotion.

plateaus: wide, flat areas of land that are surrounded by lower land.

prophet: a person who speaks for God.

rally: a large meeting.

refining: removing unwanted things from oil or other substances.

republic: a country where political power rests with the people.

ruins: what is left of something after it has fallen down.

sanctions: actions taken by a nation(s) to punish a country that has broken international law. Limits are often put on that country's buying and selling of goods and on any outside contact.

savannas: dry grasslands.

settlements: small communities set up by people from other lands or areas.

terraces: a raised, flat bank of earth with sloping sides.

terrorists: people who use violence to try to make people do what they say.

traditional: relating to ideas, beliefs, or customs that are passed down from one generation to the next.

United Nations: an international group with members from most countries of the world. It promotes understanding and peace and helps countries grow.

More Books to Read

Cooking the North African Way. Mary Winget (Lerner Publications)

I Wonder Why The Sahara is Cold at Night: And Other Questions About Deserts. I Wonder Why series. Jackie Gaff (Kingfisher)

Libya in Pictures. Visual Geography series. (Lerner Publications)

Muslim Mosque. Places of Worship series. Angela Wood (Gareth Stevens)

Peoples of the Desert. Peoples and Their Environments series. Robert Low (Rosen Publishing Group)

Phoenicians. Cultures of the Past series. Elsa Marston (Marshall Cavendish)

The Sahara Desert: The Biggest Desert. Great Record Breakers in Nature series. Aileen Weintraub (PowerKids Press)

Videos

Folk Music of the Sahara: Among the Tuareg of Libya. (Sublime Frequencies)

Sahara — A Place of Extremes. (PBS Home Video)

Web Sites

ourworld.compuserve.com/homepages/ dr_ibrahim_ighneiwa/culture.htm

www.alnpete.co.uk/lepcis/

www.holidays.net/ramadan/

www.libyana.org/

www.settlement.org/cp/english/libya/

yahooligans.yahoo.com/Around_the_ World /Countries/Libya/

Due to the dynamic nature of the Internet, some web sites stay current longer than others. To find additional web sites, use a reliable search engine with one or more of the following keywords to help you locate information about Libya. Keywords: *Bikku Bitti, Lepcis, Sabratha, Septimius Severus, Tripoli, Tuareg.*

Index